W9-CDV-777

RUNNING THE
DISTANCE

by Jared S. Blank

International Dyslexia Association
Baltimore, MD

Running the Distance
Copyright © 2019 The International Dyslexia Association, Inc.

All rights reserved. No part of this book may be reproduced, distributed, or transmitted in any form or by any electronic or mechanical means, including information storage and retrieval systems, without permission in writing from the publisher, except in the case of brief quotations embodied in reviews and certain other non-commercial uses permitted by copyright law.

Publisher's Cataloging-In-Publication Data
(Prepared by The Donohue Group, Inc.)

Names: Blank, Jared S., 1982- author.
Title: Running the distance / by Jared S. Blank.
Description: Baltimore, MD : International Dyslexia Association, [2019]
Identifiers: ISBN 9780892140701 (hardcover) | ISBN 9780892140725 (softcover) | ISBN 9780892140718 (ebook)
Subjects: LCSH: Blank, Jared S., 1982- | Dyslexics--Biography. | Male long-distance runners--Biography. | Dyslexia--Popular works. | Dyslexic children--Education--Popular works. | LCGFT: Autobiographies.
Classification: LCC RC394.W6 B53 2019 (print) | LCC RC394.W6 (ebook) | DDC 362.19685530092 B--dc23

Editing by Denise Douce, International Dyslexia Association
Cover Design and Inside Illustrations by Ryan Magsino, Vadela
Cover Photography by Molly Stark Blank, StarkLight Photography
Composition by Sara Forhan, Mid-Atlantic Design & Print, Inc.
Printed in the United States of America by Lightning Source, Ingram Content Group

Published by International Dyslexia Association

International
DYSLE✗IA
Association®

40 York Road, 4th Floor
Baltimore, MD 21204-5202
Telephone: (410) 296-0232
(800) ABC-D123
www.DyslexiaIDA.org

This book was written for the people out there who are dealing with learning challenges. I know how hard it can be, so I took on this project to help others and remind them that they are not alone. I was fortunate at a young age to have a conversation with a grad student with dyslexia. That conversation had a tremendous impact on my life, more than I realized at the time. That conversation, coupled with the support of my parents and family, helped me discover that overcoming challenges is really an opportunity. I am truly indebted to them. I share my story as a way to thank them and to advocate for others.

CONTENTS

FOREWORD

Who could possibly want to take on the World Marathon Challenge—seven marathons on seven continents in seven days? And why?

Over the course of two years, I have come to know Jared as an unassuming hero who is kind and generous, and who has a distinctive enthusiasm for life. His disarming smile, wicked sense of humor, and sparkle in his eye sets anyone in his company at ease.

Jared's story transcends the personal. The vision, determination, and courage he mustered to conquer a challenge shared by so many, won my true respect and admiration. You see, Jared is dyslexic. Overcoming the obstacles that dyslexia placed in his way required tremendous stamina and perseverance, the precise qualities that we all need to run the distance in life!

As a teacher I marvel at the innate curiosity that my young students bring to the classroom. Their insatiable appetite for knowledge is the impetus for learning. But what if the key to learning, in this case literacy, does not come easily? What if a diagnosis of dyslexia gets in the way?

If this book has caught your attention, you may have experienced the multitude of painful feelings and struggles that accompany a learning difference, be supporting someone who has dyslexia, or are wondering how to be an effective advocate. Regardless of the reason, reading Jared's inspiring account of excelling, despite the odds, is like having your own champion and personal coach in your corner! Jared digs deep and opens up to share a story that is raw, heartfelt, and poignant. He tells it through the lens and mindset of a dedicated athlete who has learned lessons through sport, in particular, collegiate football and his first love, ultramarathon running.

Which brings me back to the World Marathon Challenge, and why Jared took on this grueling feat. In accepting this quest, he saw an opportunity to combine his love of running with an issue close to his heart. He chose the International Dyslexia Association's TeamQuest fundraising platform to shine a spotlight on learning differences and bring attention to his personal mission—to change the culture of how people with dyslexia are treated in classrooms across the country and around the world.

I had the privilege of cheering Jared across the finish line at the end of the second marathon in Cape Town, South Africa. Representing his many supporters reminded me of just how many compassionate individuals it takes to support a student's success. Observing Jared's physical exhaustion as he crossed that line brought to mind the grit and effort it takes to face each day and pursue one's personal best: his smile of satisfaction upon finishing reminded me that it is always worth the effort!

To anyone doing something difficult—this book is for you. You are not alone!

Jane Cooper
Teacher
President, IDA – Oregon Branch
August 2019

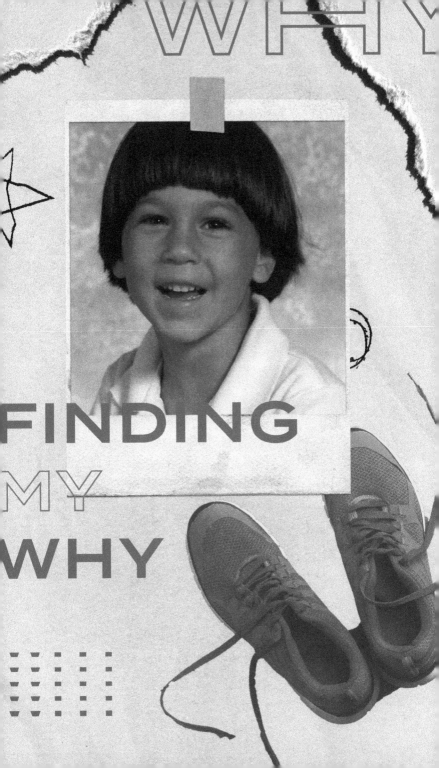

WHY

FINDING

MY

WHY

"The next eighteen years of your life will be like running with a cut on the bottom of your foot," my doctor told me. "You can do it, but it will be painful."

FINDING MY WHY

At a young age, I overheard someone telling my parents that I probably wouldn't graduate from high school. Although my parents knew better than to accept this judgment without question, for me, those words were devastating. I could already tell that I wasn't like everyone else. I was having trouble learning to read. As it turns out, I had dyslexia, and I still do.

You might be wondering how someone with dyslexia ends up writing a book about running seven marathons on seven continents in seven days. It wasn't easy, but for me, learning challenges are a chance to turn obstacles into opportunities. Whenever I had to do something difficult, or someone told me I couldn't do something, I did it anyway.

Years ago, I learned that happiness, while nice, is simply a byproduct. It is not a goal. Working hard to accomplish goals that I care about makes me happy. It's why I find joy in learning and running, even when they are hard, and I feel overwhelmed. In those moments, I grow; I find ways to figure things out. I improve and happiness follows.

Throughout my life, knowing that I am not alone has been critical to my happiness. Therefore, helping others also makes me happy. Individuals with learning challenges—and their loved ones—need to know they are not alone. I have been fortunate to have a supportive family help me get to this point. But what about all of those who lack the necessary support system? Like other challenges I have faced in life, I knew that writing a book wouldn't be easy. But I'm doing it because I hope that sharing my challenges and experiences will help others like me and make them feel less alone.

SOME-
THING
WRONG

FAILING

NAP

TIME

My world did not

make sense.

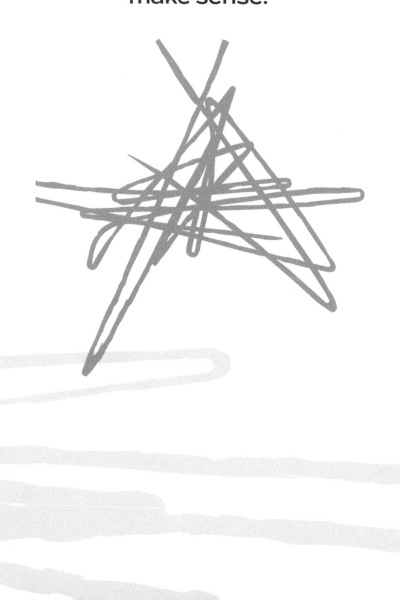

FAILING NAP TIME

I was five years old the first time that I remember feeling like something was wrong. I was with the eye doctor. I knew there was an issue, but I couldn't articulate what it was. But I knew.

It was as if my heart and brain had conferred and agreed that something was off. Sitting in that office, the eye doctor told me she wanted to bring my mother, Lynn, into the room. I was sitting in the examination chair. My heart was racing, my face flushed. I began to realize that others were starting to guess what I had already figured out—something was wrong with me.

When I tried to read the eye chart, the one with all the rows of letters, the doctor said *seeing* the board was not the problem. It was recognizing and deciphering the letters. This made sense to me because my glasses weren't helping; they only caused headaches.

Then I heard the word that would become such an important part of my life: *dyslexia*. The doctor thought I had it. My mother, an educator, understood the diagnosis. Something had always seemed off to her. She had watched me struggle with simple tasks like writing letters with a pencil or working on art projects.

After the visit with my eye doctor I went through a series of tests to pinpoint the problem. I traveled to Torrance, California, to visit specialists at the Jean Ayres Clinic. The initial diagnosis was confirmed: I was dyslexic. I also had a sensory processing disorder, which contributes to learning challenges and affects fine motor skills.

What exactly does that mean? Well, things that are easy for most people—holding a pencil, using scissors, tying shoes—were excruciating for me. A classroom example would go something like this: The teacher would ask us to draw an image of a favorite thing. An idea would materialize in my head. I knew exactly what it should look like, but when it was time to put it on paper, I couldn't do it.

In school, these difficulties were already apparent in kindergarten. In fact, I had to repeat kindergarten to try to catch up. I felt like I was already becoming a statistic—someone who wouldn't amount to anything.

When I tell people that I had to repeat kindergarten, they don't believe me at first. They ask, "What happened?" or "Did you fail nap time?" or "How does anyone flunk out of kindergarten?" I have to explain that even though the teacher would say there is no wrong way to complete an art project, I still found a way to mess it up. But I learned that it helps to stay positive. So, when I'm asked about failing and repeating kindergarten, I simply say, "I can find a way to do anything." That idea continues to give me strength. It is a source of power for me.

During my second year of kindergarten, the teacher presented us with half of an image. We were instructed to complete the image by drawing in the other half. I found myself looking at half of a coffee cup, the side with the handle. I had a hard time processing what I should draw, so I took the assignment a little too literally. In my head, if you only have half a coffee cup, the other half of the image would show coffee spilling out the other side. I shaded the other half of the paper with black to represent the spilled coffee.

The teacher was not amused. She didn't think I was taking the project seriously, so I was punished, forced to stay inside during recess to redraw the image—a complete coffee cup—but I couldn't do it.

It was frustrating. My world did not make sense. I did not belong, and I did not want to be in that class.

Later, when my report card arrived, I assumed it would reflect my struggle. But the same teacher who made me stay inside during recess said I was thriving in the classroom. That's a great thing to tell your parents, but I was confused. Was I performing well in class or not?

My mom was confused too. She wasn't seeing the academic progress expected in a child my age, so she decided to investigate further by checking in with my teacher. Again, the teacher confirmed I was doing well.

Another week passed before the teacher conferred with an aide and realized that I was having trouble. At that point she called my mother. Looking back, I don't think my teacher was invested in my performance. She clearly did not remember or know how I was really doing in the classroom.

Once my teacher realized her mistake, she asked us to return the report card so she could change the marks to sub-satisfactory! My mom refused. She did not want me reduced to a forgotten mark on a piece of paper.

But I had other issues, too.

I needed help developing the most basic, everyday skills: writing with a pencil, tying my shoes. I spent hours and hours in occupational therapy, learning how to function in the world. For example, to improve my fine motor skills and strengthen my hands, I used my fingers to draw in a sandbox or on a table covered with shaving cream.

Balancing myself so I could sit in a chair was also a struggle. For me, this meant working with balancing equipment, which is very similar to improving core strength at the gym. I also had to sit on a swing, spin around, and stand up to regain balance—an exercise that often left me nauseated and disoriented. In fact, everything in occupational therapy was a challenge. But it helped that I had support from my family, instructors, and coaches; they did not let me quit and walk away. They reminded me that although my hands were not working, there were other ways that I could move forward and improve. It was like having a crew at an ultramarathon; they would not let me stop.

I've also learned from the experiences of others. One day, my Uncle Miles took me on a car ride. He was recovering from a stroke. We shared our challenges. It was a lesson in empathy for me as I watched him limp in and out of the car. He refused to give up despite obvious challenges. He was making the best life that he possibly could. It really inspired me. It was like a seed had been sown in me; one I have been nurturing ever since.

It also helped to know that I could throw and kick a ball with precision. I was proud of that. I kept telling myself that I could do those things well. As long as someone could open the car door for me, tie my shoes, and get me to the soccer field, I could take care of the rest. I could play. And, in those moments, dyslexia couldn't slow me down. There was no disability. I wasn't different. I was just another athlete—and I valued that immensely.

As I worked on my physical struggles, I still had a lot of work to do academically. My parents hired a tutor, or, as I called it, "school on top of school." I would go to school in the morning, work my way through those academic challenges, and then go home for more "school" at night. It wasn't all bad, though. One of my tutors, Paige Chandler (we still keep in touch), drove a convertible. Quite frankly, she was a badass. She told my parents that I seemed sad, quiet, and depressed. I was only seven years old! But she was right. My hands did not work right. I could not grasp school and I knew it; that was the worst part about it. I was watching students achieve and succeed in school, but I wasn't close to doing that, and I didn't know why.

However, I wasn't jealous of my classmates. I was always genuinely excited for people and their successes—I wanted others to win. But I wanted to be able to produce and show what I could do as well. Instead, I was behind. I wanted to compete against the best to get better. But I was so far behind, my only competition was with myself. So, I decided to become the best version of myself. What is the most I can learn, do, and achieve? Of course, at seven years of age, I still had a long way to go.

Dyslexia is like a race—you need a strategy. If you don't have a plan to win, you will lag behind and soon be out of the race.

LAGGING BEHIND

My life as an elementary school student started early in the morning. I practiced spelling with my mom before school. She taught me to count words on my hand. For example, to learn the word *prepare*, I would count three letters (*p-r-e*) on my left hand and four letters (*p-a-r-e*) on my right, which made it easier for me to work with each segment of the word. After that early morning practice with my mom, I would go to school for half the morning to take my spelling test. My mom's strategy almost worked perfectly, except that on one of my tests I reversed the count on my hands. Instead of spelling *prepare*, I spelled *parepre*.

Fortunately, my second-grade teacher, Mrs. Gronquist, was compassionate. She drew some arrows to correct what I had done and gave me credit (thanks, Mrs. Gronquist!). After the spelling test, I would go to occupational therapy. There was so little time that I ate part of my lunch during the drive to Emanuel Hospital on the other side of town.

In my occupational therapy sessions, I was put in a swing and strategically spun around. To this day, I still don't understand why, but I went through many tests and experiments as a kid that didn't make sense to me. I just kept my head down.

After occupational therapy, I tried to finish my lunch, still nauseated from the spinning. Then, it was one more cross-town trip back to school to finish the day. I missed lunch with friends and recess on the playground. This probably delayed some of my social and emotional growth. I didn't know what to tell the other kids when they asked: What was I doing? Where was I going? How does a second grader explain that to another second grader? I didn't. I was too embarrassed.

Things were better after school. I got to play soccer before more tutoring, and I definitely enjoyed soccer more than tutoring. Actually, that's all I really wanted to do—play soccer. Playing sports was one of the few times life actually made any sense to me. When I was moving around with a ball, nothing else existed and that was great for me. But my parents have always believed in education. My mother is an educator and my father is a lawyer. They kept reminding me that I could accomplish my academic goals with the right training. Although I dreamed of training to be a soccer player, the practices and games would come to an end, and it was back to the tutors. So, I was really training to be a student—even though that was much more difficult for me.

With my parents' support, I was able to face my weakest areas head on. Through it all, they never put pressure on me. Instead, they provided the tools and opportunities I needed to succeed. They were always all in—even when people told them to lower their expectations.

By third grade, my parents were attending Individualized Education Program (IEP) meetings at my school. These meetings included many education advisors and experts such as principals, administrators, education specialists, and teachers. These meetings resulted in a plan that included accommodations to help me in areas where I was struggling. For example, I was given extra time to take exams. Also, during these meetings, the education specialist would give his or her overall assessment of me. To this day, I remember that in one of these meetings someone told my parents I might not graduate high school and to not expect higher than C grades from me. My parents did not agree. They felt that the educator could not give a proper assessment as he certainly did not know me very well. The words from the specialist stayed with me though. It was like carrying a backpack with weights or walking with a massive cut on your foot— it's hard to shake that nagging at the back of your mind throughout the day.

Elementary school also presented me with some logistical challenges. Aside from going to the Emanuel Hospital for occupational therapy, I was also supposed to go to the resource room for special education at school. They called it the *resource room* to avoid the stigma associated with the term *special education.* But kids catch on quick, and everyone knew. I remember telling the librarian that I would be going to the resource room instead of the library, and she got very angry at me. I believe someone forgot to tell her about my IEP. She kept driving home the idea that reading was an important subject. Looking back, I definitely agree with her, but I couldn't read the books, and I didn't know how to properly convey this to her at such a young age. Moreover, I just couldn't seem to win. If I stayed in the library, the librarian was happy, but the resource room teacher was angry. In other words, it didn't really matter where I spent my time, because at the end of the day, I was still struggling in school.

Eventually, the discussion in the IEP meetings changed enough that the school tried to tell my parents that I didn't have any issues, and they essentially had no responsibility to help me. My parents had to fight very hard with the school system to convince them that dyslexia was an issue and that I had it. They were relentless in their efforts. When I look back on everything my parents went through to show the school officials that dyslexia was real, I am inspired and so grateful and impressed. Many people told them that everything would be okay; they just needed to be patient and wait and see. But my parents knew better. They knew that learning challenges do not get better over time without training. Dyslexia is like a race—you need a strategy. If you don't have a plan to win, you will lag behind and soon be out of the race.

I desperately wanted to stay in the race. And, I was willing to work hard. But it helps to have hope too. Once again, knowing that I was not alone really helped. One time that I remember feeling that way was when my grandma asked the neighbor's grandson to talk to me. He told me all about how he was getting his master's degree. He admitted that it was very hard, but it was doable, even though he had dyslexia. This gave me hope. If someone else could do it, so could I. It seemed worth the effort to stay in the race.

As fifth grade came to an end, my parents and I had to decide which school I would attend next. I did not know it at the time, but this decision would spark a fire in me.

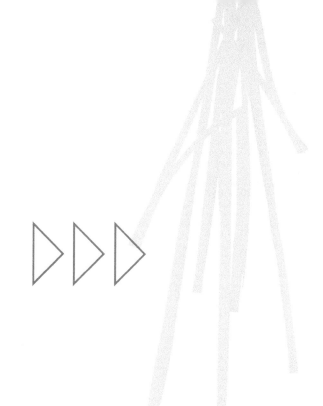

I began to understand
that facing challenges
was making me stronger.

04:00:00

CHALLENGE ACCEPTED

As I neared the end of fifth grade, my teachers recommended that my parents and I look for an alternative to West Sylvan, the typical choice for middle school in the area. They found an independent school for students with learning challenges. I was on board with it initially because I knew that I needed additional learning support. However, it turned out that the new school was not the right fit for me.

I do believe there are some really good independent schools for students with dyslexia; but, at this school, I felt isolated, as if I did not belong. Unlike many of the students there who had multiple learning challenges, I could comprehend the material with some accommodations, such as help from a notetaker, extra time, and a quiet space to take my tests.

A third of the way into the school year, I came to the conclusion that the independent school was not going to work for me. I feared that I was falling even further behind. I wanted to compete with the neurotypical students. Not only was I not competing with them, I believed that I was outclassed by them. But I was not likely to get the support I needed at West Sylvan. What do you do when you only have two options, and you know neither one will work? Which do you choose?

I became even more frustrated when it came to the one area I did enjoy—sports. The kids that I played sports with went to one school, and I went to another. At soccer practices they all wore their school logo. I pretended everything was okay, but it was not. I felt lost.

But I was very lucky, because at difficult times like this, family, friends, and others offered to help. This time it was my brother Adam. He told me that if I wanted to change schools, first I had to show that I could do the work. Even if I felt it was "beneath me," I had to do the work. Thanks to his advice, I learned there is no work too small or insignificant; the challenge is to take the task assigned and do it to the best of my ability—no matter how I feel about it emotionally. I reflect on this feeling a lot today, and I believe it has helped me throughout my life.

By the final quarter of that first year at the independent school, I stopped thinking about where I was in my overall progress and began to focus only on what the teachers were asking me to do. When I got home from practice, I did my schoolwork to the best of my ability. Toward the end of the year, I calmly told my parents that I was not performing at a high enough level where I was, and that I was not getting better or more proficient. To a certain extent they agreed, so we were able to start a conversation about shifting my educational strategy.

We decided that West Sylvan would be the best option for my middle school, albeit with some conditions. My parents convinced the school to give me regular classes along with some individual one-on-one tutoring time, which my parents would provide (at a significant financial cost to them).

Margaret McNabb was a dynamic teacher at my old school; she was someone I really learned from and trusted. Her teaching style, partnered with my strong work ethic, resulted in significant academic improvement for me. My parents saw this and hired her to be my tutor. I was so excited to have her join the team. I always compare it to when Shaquille O'Neal was signed away by the Lakers; Margaret was that great! I was getting a shot to compete—a shot to prove myself.

But I still had a long way to go. I thought that the academics at West Sylvan would be the biggest challenge I would face, but it was much more than that. It was how I felt about myself. Because I had so many educational needs, I convinced myself that I was actually stupid. No matter how much I tried, I still needed help, and that reaffirmed my belief that I was dumb. Working with a tutor felt very isolating, so it might have helped if I had known others like me. Instead, I felt alone—both physically and emotionally.

I was, however, beginning to make some progress in the classroom. And, once I started getting As, it helped me reevaluate my intelligence. Of course, now, as an adult, I understand that grades aren't necessarily an indicator of intelligence. But back then, it was the only measure I knew, so falling short on my grades was a huge setback. I remember getting a B+ in science and trying to convince the teacher to give me an A-. I fought hard for it; I felt as if my life depended on it.

It was as though that one change would make me feel smart and convince the teacher too.

By eighth grade, I felt as though a beast was waking up inside of me. It seemed to be getting stronger and stronger now that grades started to matter. So, I concentrated my efforts on academics and sports. I was enjoying being a kid and had some time for friends, but I was very clear on my priorities.

High school was approaching, and we would need to pick another school. Lincoln was definitely my first choice. My soccer coach was the coach there, and I really wanted to play for him, but I agreed to visit and interview at a few other schools. The interviews went well, but I wasn't accepted, most likely because I said I didn't like to read. When I was not accepted into any of the private schools, my decision was basically made for me. I was going to Lincoln High School. It was a great feeling to finally go to a school where I wanted to be, even though I knew it would be a challenge. But this time I was ready. I was still very young, but I already had faced many challenges—and I was beginning to understand that facing them was making me stronger.

GET IT

PERSONAL

BEST

When you continue to apply these lessons to whatever the future brings you, you will knock it out of the ball park.

DONE

To be our best,

we have to do the best

with what we have.

PERSONAL BEST

Finishing eighth grade, my academics were more or less in order, but it didn't take long before I was feeling lost in the classroom. I had just started high school, and I was already three weeks behind! Were the people right who questioned if I would graduate from high school?

One thing I have learned from the many learning specialists I have seen over the years is that for every hour that a neurotypical student spends on homework or classwork, I would have to spend about three hours for the same output. In other words, it would take me significantly longer than most students to do my assignments, and, if I wanted to do well, I had to accept that and commit to the work. It's one of the many ways that running marathons has helped me understand the challenges I have faced in my own life as well as those faced by others. Some people can't run as long or as fast as I do, and some can run farther and faster. I get it. I know how hard it can be. That's why all runners and people working on their fitness have my respect. I've been there. To be our best, we have to do the best with what we have.

I am so fortunate that once again my family was there to help. My mom reminded me that I had made the choice to take on this challenge, and it was my responsibility to "get it done." That talk with my mom was a turning point for me. It stoked a fire that always has been there and has fueled my ability to keep trying and moving forward. I still felt lost and overwhelmed, but I knew that to get what I wanted in life, I would need to figure it out.

I talked to Mom about the problems I was having at the start of ninth grade. I began to set goals. I was determined to prove the classroom evaluators wrong. To do that, I decided that I needed a 4.0 grade point average, a letter in soccer, and the title of senior class president. That weekend, I studied the longest I ever had on my own. I studied about three hours before my tutoring session (in high school I worked with a tutor every weekend). My tutor was impressed! After the session, I went home and did more work on my own. I learned that if I worked three hours on my own, I could push myself to study even more because I was feeling more prepared and encouraged by the results that I was seeing.

Still, one thing that distanced me from my peers and the "normal" high school experience was my daily trip to the resource room. Anyone who had any type of "disability" went to that room. I knew people were talking about me and wondering why I went there. Why couldn't I just be like everyone else for once?

Typically, I went to the resource room to get my assignments, and then I would walk to another room to meet with my tutor. But I began to wonder if there might be a way to change that. Unlike my peers, my IEP allowed me to skip a foreign language—but I really wanted to take one for two reasons. First, I would be starting at the same time and level as everyone else. It would give me a chance to prove that my hard work was enough to distance myself from average. Second, if I could substitute the foreign language class for the resource room period, I would be in a "regular" room learning a new language—the same thing every other student would be doing.

The extra time studying became critical when taking a foreign language. I used it for *rote learning*, a memorization technique based on repetition.

I designed a schedule and followed it strictly. During the week, I woke up, went to school, attended soccer practice, then completed my homework—and sometimes after that, I had tutoring in the evenings for two to three hours. On weekends, I managed to study six hours per day. I also played recreational basketball on the weekends, so I would knock out a few hours of studying before the game and then finished the rest when I returned home. If I had friends over on the weekends, I would wake up before them and study. I even snuck away to work on a paper while they played video games at night. It was like a game to me. I didn't want to be behind, so I was willing to put in the work, no matter what the cost. This routine only grew more intense, especially after I started seeing results.

By the end of freshman year, I had a perfect grade point average and the conversation about my future had changed. I first noticed the change when Mrs. Pat Walker, the resource teacher, came to me before my annual year-end IEP meeting and asked me which schools I was considering for college. I had not even thought about college at this point! To be honest, I didn't think it was an option for me. I also didn't know many colleges. In fact, the only ones I could mention were prominent schools in the National Collegiate Athletic Association (NCAA) Basketball Tournament (growing up, I really loved watching that tournament): North Carolina, Michigan, and Duke. They were great basketball schools, but also respected academic institutions. Unfortunately, even though my grades were perfect, my standardized test scores were below average. Those scores broke my heart, because they seemed to confirm that I wasn't as smart as my grade point average. It fed into my fear that I was stupid, and I was afraid that it would make it even harder to prove that I wasn't. So, I worked even harder.

Sophomore year I had a perfect grade point average and was on the junior varsity soccer team. I was achieving my goals! I kept up with my study regimen and was trying to incorporate more of a social life. But it wasn't easy. Once a week, I attended Jewish school and sophomore year was the confirmation trip to Washington, D.C., with some of my classmates. The last thing I wanted was to seem disrespectful toward my culture, but I did not want to go because it was time away from my regular school and days without studying. I felt as though it would put me even farther behind.

One day, the administrator of the Jewish school, who was a very nice person, tried to talk me into going on the trip. I remember the conversation—she knew it would be tough for me to leave school in the midst of classes, but she thought the experience would be important. Ultimately, I agreed and went on the trip. She was right; I had a great time and I learned a lot about myself. Most of our time on the trip was in a social setting, and I realized that being dyslexic did not hold me back at all in those situations.

When the trip was over, my mind was immediately back on school. Before I left for D.C. I had performed poorly on a Spanish test. At the time, my teacher told me I could make up the test and retake it the week after my trip to D.C., but I declined because I thought the teacher was giving me special treatment. Instead, I made up my mind to perform better for the rest of the semester. My Grandma Fay would have been so mad at me for this decision. She encouraged me to use every advantage I could get. But I didn't that time, and, consequently, I finished the first semester of my sophomore year with all As except for a B in Spanish. Because my ultimate goal was all As, I saw anything less as a fail, which I know now was not really the case.

If you try your best, then the grades are what they are. The lesson here is that it doesn't pay to punish yourself: by not retaking the Spanish test, I fell short on my goals and didn't give myself the best chance to succeed.

Getting that B in Spanish class crushed me. All of the anger and frustration from thinking I was stupid and dumb escalated when I received that grade. It seemed to validate my worst fears. It didn't help that some of my teachers still did not understand that dyslexia was an actual thing and that some people needed extra time on tests. The fight for accommodations and recognition of dyslexia was still hard to come by. Teachers would look at me and conclude "nothing looks wrong with you." They would not believe me until they saw my IEP. It made me so angry that I stopped talking to people over winter break. All I wanted to do was go for runs and hit the weight room. Being in motion helped me tremendously in coping with anger and frustration.

After blowing my pristine grade point average, I started the second semester of my sophomore year with renewed determination. I was completely focused on getting back on track academically. I committed fully to school and sports. When we went on spring break,

I took all of my books, woke up early, and started each day by studying or working on a paper. I felt confident that my hard work and meticulous research would pay off with my paper, but when I came back from break my tutor told me that I still wasn't quite "getting it." So, all that work had to be redone. I was upset. It felt like a waste of work. Nonetheless, I would not leave the table until it was right. The hours were stacking up at this point. I was now working three hours each weeknight, a little before school, and on Fridays when I usually took a break unless I had final exams. Friday was now my kickstart study day into the weekend.

I finished the year back at the top with a perfect grade point average. The difference this time was that I did not care as much about the grade point average. Make no mistake, I still wanted it, but I cared more about managing the anger and frustration that I had when others thought my failure was inevitable. Maybe this was a new passion that could help me succeed— *proving others wrong.*

Junior year started the same way that my sophomore year had ended: I was on fire. My grades were perfect, and I felt like momentum was on my side. I needed to keep it up, though, and with that came a lot of strategic thinking and giving myself even more time for studying. I convinced my parents that I could no longer attend Jewish school; I needed that day. One of the more difficult things I had to forego was attending Blazer games with my dad. Having only one professional sports team in Portland, Oregon, these games were a big deal to us and one of the things I really enjoyed doing. I had to stop going because my schoolwork was piling up, and I needed to focus. Basically, if something in my life was not a school event, workout, practice, game, or track meet, it was not on my schedule.

I remember one time, after a recreational basketball game, my teammates were going to the beach. I was invited, but I gave them some excuse like my parents would not let me go. They knew better. My friends were accepting and understanding, but they could tell it was my decision and that my parents were not standing in the way. They knew me well enough to understand what I was battling, and they were supportive.

I still tried to go to as many school events as I could because I wanted to be senior class president. During freshman year, I had sometimes stayed late to clean graffiti for extra credit from my biology teacher. After a while I did it for more reasons than just extra credit. I felt as though I wanted to give something back to the school, and I liked the challenge of figuring out how to remove the most stubborn marks.

Academically, I was in a good place but couldn't stop thinking about athletics either. I was trying very hard to improve my soccer ability. I played on three teams outside of school by mid-junior year because I was so determined to make varsity. But as much as I loved soccer, and it was a great release, I came to realize that I was limited as a player. My effort was the only thing that really set me apart on the field. I could give the same output for long periods of time. Long after I moved on from soccer, this ability would continue to serve me well in many other pursuits. But for now, my life was school, studying, and sports.

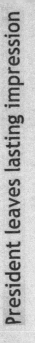
President leaves lasting impression

Run Jared, Run: Senior Class president Jared ...k runs through the hall on a daily mission.

MY
ULTRABEST

" I learned the three C's being Senior Class president: compromise, communicate, an connect.

Jared Blank
Senior Class President

The more perfectly I could do things, the more evidence there would be that I was not stupid.

At the end of my junior year, I learned that I had been elected senior class president! While I knew this new role would be exciting and fulfilling, I had to focus even more of my attention in planning for the next school year as president. Of course, I still wanted to achieve my goal of making the varsity soccer team too. And, after a summer of training, I really had improved my fitness. During tryouts we had a twelve-minute Cooper test where you are supposed to run as long as you can for twelve minutes. Elite soccer athletes can usually run two miles in twelve minutes. I trained hard for that test because I knew that distance running was mainly about effort. I completed more than eight laps during the test, which is more than two miles. As a freshman, I had passed out during physical education class attempting to run one six-minute mile, and now I was doing two miles at that pace! I made the team! Going into my senior year, I was class president and a member of the varsity soccer team, and, for the most part, I had perfect grades (I still cringe at that Spanish grade). I felt confident applying to numerous colleges.

I kept up my studying regimen, but something was changing: my ability to handle work was increasing, and I was getting stronger and executing better. I was no longer building skill; I was operating like a finely tuned machine. When you train for distance races there are different phases. In the base building phase, you run miles to get a foundation. Once the foundation is solid, you train on a track, running faster paces. That's the speed work phase. The third phase is maintenance, where you hold the current level you have achieved with your training. My academic studies in my senior year were a lot like that as well. Even though I was busy doing more with school because of my duties as president, the difference was that I wasn't fighting or struggling to keep myself in the game like I had been during my sophomore and junior years. I was "in the flow," as they say.

Soccer was going well. Our team made it to the state playoffs that year, and I played in enough games to receive a letter for the year. By the end of high school, I was doing a good job of balancing school and sports. I was achieving my goals.

The second semester of high school was flying by, and I was able to maintain my deliberate focus on my goals. But it was almost time to pick a college—I was closing in on uncharted waters. My fears of not graduating resurfaced. The self-doubt that had haunted me since childhood had returned. I had three mindsets when considering the next phase of my life. First, part of me did not want more time in school. I thought anything would be better. While probably not fair to compare, I thought about Kobe Bryant and how jealous I was of him going straight from high school to the professional world. I figured if I could just get started in the workforce, I would be better off. Second, the other part of me thought that if my two older brothers went to college, so could I. That was the side of me that still had something to prove. Lastly, I wanted to work in sports and being at a school in Los Angeles might help me get that opportunity.

Realistically, I didn't have the option to play professional sports straight out of high school. I think it's good to have a dream, but sometimes reality interferes with those dreams. Fortunately, I wasn't too disappointed. I knew I could still do something in sports. Looking back now, I needed to prove to myself and others that I could do it. The more perfectly I could do it (for example, all As), the more evidence there would be that I was not stupid. This level of perfectionism probably helped me develop the drive and skills I needed to succeed. But I would learn later that accepting myself for who I am keeps the focus on where I really want to go, rather than what others expect of me.

I finished the soccer season and earned the title of most inspirational player. I also finished track while competing in districts at the varsity level, earning a second letter and the most inspirational award. People on the track team projected that I would run marathons one day—something at the time I thought was foolish. In school, I graduated as salutatorian with all As and one B and had a few other awards such as being elected prom king and speaking at graduation. I got into most of the schools I applied to and even earned scholarships from a few. Imagine—the kid who had been told he probably wouldn't graduate high school, graduated with honors and had a choice of colleges!

...ity by virtue of the authority vested
...mmendation of the faculty of

...duate School

...ferred the degree of

...ster of Arts
...cation Management

...on

...ed S. Blank

...rnia, on the seventh day of August, in the year
...e thousand and seven.

Jean Morrison
Vice Provost for Graduate Programs

COLLEGE

DAYS

USC

RUN
RUN
RUN

...ar Jared,
...u should be extremely proud of yourself for
... incredible effort for an incredible journey,
...t just the physical piece—as this took as
...uch brain power as it did leg power.

Sometimes things go wrong,

but sometimes they go right.

It helps to remember that

when you are discouraged.

When I talk to students now, I challenge them to make decisions based on their strengths and passions rather than trying to prove something to themselves or others. A few of the small schools would have probably suited me best and allowed me to play sports at the Division III level, but I was still trying to prove myself. Despite all of my achievements, none of them mattered when it came to how I felt about myself. I still believed that others saw me as less intelligent and less of a person, and I wanted to prove them wrong. There is a scene in the film *Good Will Hunting* where the main character has to choose to be beaten by either a belt, wrench, or stick. He knows that any of the options will hurt, so why not pick the most painful? It is the best preparation for moving forward. Picking a college was similar to that for me. If I was going to put myself through the hard work of college, I might as well do it on the highest level with the most challenging academic conditions that I could find.

So, I chose to go to the University of Southern California (USC), knowing it was going to be incredibly challenging.

Freshman year, if I wasn't in class, or practicing, or competing in cross country club, I was in the dorm studying. I hardly ever left the room for social activities. Some of the same study methods that I used in high school, for example, rote learning—one of my extreme memorization tactics—wasn't as useful in college. The questions on the practice tests were very different than the material I had memorized. I could read, but I didn't understand what I was reading in a way that would help me do well on tests. I had accommodations in college, extra time for tests and notetakers, but I still wasn't doing as well as I thought I should.

Running was critical in college because it was the only time I took a break from work. By winter break, my grades were As and Bs, which was not acceptable for my standards, but I understood that college was much harder than high school, and I was somewhat okay with it. My running was improving, and I went with a group to the mountain to build mileage and train at different altitudes.

In the spring, I was still studying and running all of the time. Although I loved learning new things, I was not enjoying school. I told myself that college was dumb; I felt burned out, but I kept going because I was on a mission to prove myself. It didn't help that I hurt myself in the spring during track. It felt like a major setback. Although I was still busy with rehab and cross training, it was not the same as running. I could not focus on anything. The injury lingered into my sophomore year.

Joining a fraternity helped in some ways. My brothers had both been at Alpha Epsilon Pi (AEPi), a Jewish fraternity, and since I could not run because of my injury, I thought it would be good to be doing something besides just studying all the time. Even though I was not really in a state to connect with others because I missed training so much, it did help. The guys were awesome and made me feel welcome, even though I was not a party person.

I'm glad that I was a part of my biological brothers' brotherhood as a legacy, but as it turned out, I did not spend that much time with them. I needed the time to study, and I was struggling with my major in kinesiology; I was having trouble with the sciences. My writing, on the other hand, was actually getting better. Unlike high school, I did well in classes that required papers rather than tests.

Although this was a challenging time for me, I realized that so many had it much worse. I was thankful to have had such loving and supportive friends and family. It may seem like I had everything figured out, but I didn't. And, I hope that knowing you are not alone will help you as much as it has helped me. Sometimes things go wrong, but sometimes they go right. It helps to always remember that when you feel discouraged.

FROM
COLLEGE TO
REAL WORLD

**Each experience...
helped me clarify
and add to the
list of goals I was
beginning to have
for my career.**

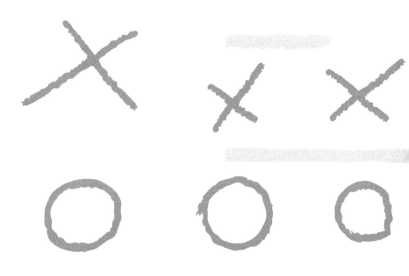

FROM COLLEGE TO REAL WORLD

With the help of my dad, I took some time to regroup during the summer between sophomore and junior year. I asked him what he thought about all the times people had told him that I would be limited in terms of what I was capable of accomplishing. Specifically, we talked about being told that I would not get grades above a C. He said, "They don't know your parents, and they certainly do not know my son!" Although he was very proud of what I had accomplished with grades, he did think that I should work on my relationships with people. To help with this, he introduced me to Jon Spoelstra, a brilliant marketer and leader.

When Jon and I met at Starbucks, he suggested that I major in communications and meet with people working in sports. I was reenergized by the meeting and returned to school with a different perspective. I got a job working in the training room for the athletics department and let academics go a little bit. I didn't lose focus, but I allowed myself to experience a world beyond books and studying. I was working twenty hours a week and studying when I could. It was a new world for me.

In football, when a team is leading by enough points to get the win, that team can take a knee and let the clock run down to end the game as quickly as possible. I later learned that this is one of the best plays in sports. Essentially, I applied the same principle to my academics in college. I did enough work at the beginning and used a little strategy of changing majors (kind of like half-time adjustments) to get the job done and graduate with a degree from USC.

During my junior year, I struggled somewhat transitioning from my old, familiar habits of focusing on academics to more time working at a job. The head trainer at my college, Russ Romano, had hired me to work for the football department. As I began to gain some experience on the job, I found that I enjoyed looking at the big picture of how a football team operates and the roles of the various departments. I liked how management had the power to solve problems, position people to succeed, and make things run smoother for everyone. I began to see how I could be a part of this work.

By senior year, my focus and efforts shifted almost entirely from studying to work. I had an internship with Mark Jackson, director of football operations. He worked hand in hand with Coach Pete Carroll, and I respected the way he conducted business. Working with Mark was such a special opportunity; it shaped my view of work and what I hoped to do one day. I wanted to do what Mark was doing. Each experience, like the one with Mark, helped me clarify and add to the list of goals I was beginning to have for my career. There were some hard moments in college, but within four years, I finished with a degree and landed a job offer from USC football.

TURNING

PRO

KEEP UP

I was winless once, too, but I didn't let that stop me.

TURNING PRO

I started my full-time job two days after graduation. I remember coming into the office to help when recruits and families were visiting campus, organize information for the director of football operations, and do any task that any coach or staff person needed in the office. It was important to me that the staff knew that I had not forgotten where I came from. I also checked in with the training and equipment room staff because those departments were critical to the organization.

Most days I was running around like a madman, doing everything from carrying the water caddy to training the players. I was so busy doing different assignments throughout the day that when I was picking up lunch for a coach and he offered to buy mine, I usually passed because I was so worried about the extra time it would take. Skipping meals was a pattern for me that started in childhood. I needed every minute I could get to keep up. People would often give me a hard time about it; they did not know my history, and why eating during the day was a challenge for me. I have since learned that it is better to eat and refuel during the day.

I was also responsible for transcript evaluations. But the days were so chaotic, I had to do that work at night so I could carefully check the "b's" and "d's" to make sure they weren't reversed. The coaches worked at night as well, so I figured I should be there anyway. It was nice at night because the coaches were watching film and not asking for stuff, so I was able to finish the work that I could not get to during the day. This job taught me a lot about patience, diligence, and thoroughness. The environment was fast-paced, challenging, and exciting all at the same time. Just like in school, I had a goal to guide me: I wanted to learn the entire business of football. And, I was off to a good start. Starting in the training room, being an intern, and getting hired as a recruiting assistant were the first steps toward that goal.

Before long, I was promoted to director of player personnel. While working, I also took night classes and graduated with a master's degree in communication management. No one told me that I needed a master's degree, but I needed to prove to myself that I could do it. Before, I was trying to prove my competence to others; this time it was for me.

When USC won the Rose Bowl in 2008, I got the opportunity to move to Seattle, Washington, to be the director of player personnel for the Washington Huskies. The Huskies at the time were coming off a winless season and needed to rebuild. I did not flinch at the thought of leaving a Rose Bowl winning team to work with a winless team. I was winless once, too, and I didn't let that stop me. I could use the same drive and determination that got me through high school and college to help the Huskies find their winning stride.

My title with the Huskies was the same, but I was given more responsibility with new challenges. I had to adjust to a new environment and learn a new way of doing things with new people. What worked at one place might or might not work at another. For example, unlike where I had worked before, Washington had a facility department. I had to work with them and learn what was required for an event. It was a new experience for me, but a good one. I enjoyed learning about their needs and best practices. Once I did, I was able to make more accurate project decisions and make their jobs easier by giving them schedules in advance.

When I worked at the University of Washington, I lived with roommates near Seattle Pacific University. One of them coached there and told me about the master's in business administration (MBA) program that had flexible class schedules. I had been wanting an MBA because it would add quantitative study to my toolkit. I applied for the program and was accepted. So, on the two nights a week that I had class, I would work until 5:30 p.m., go to class from 6:00 to 9:00 p.m., and then return to work at 9:30 p.m. and work until about 11:30 p.m. I wrote papers and studied during flights to away games. I made a shift in my schedule, much like in the second part of my undergraduate study. But now, work always came first. I was still committed to spending any remaining time on schoolwork. This approach worked well for me; I graduated with an MBA in 2013.

BE THE

u have taken your challenges and turned them

:o inspiration for not only your friends and family,

t for other children, educators, athletes,

d parents too.

MENTORS

ANS

I knew if I didn't try, I would never know. The only way to find out was to take on the challenge.

10:00:00
MENTORS

Mentors have always played a critical role in my success. They helped me at the time I knew them, and their advice still guides me to this day. In high school, Mr. Bailey, my civics teacher and senior class advisor, taught me the importance of leadership. He always said, "The person in the middle gets crushed." I thought this was a great challenge. I also learned many lessons from my good friend, Mike Gotesman, who died in 2007. He had a unique way of seeing the world. I learned so much from him about empathy and patience, two things I really value in life. I've also been fortunate to have a number of mentors in my professional career.

One of those key mentors in my professional life was Pete Carroll. The entire staff called him Coach for good reason—he's one of the best ever. He taught me how to work with great intensity and hustle to get things done. He was always teaching philosophy and applying it to both football and life. One thing that Coach would say that really stuck with me was "Anyone can do it once." He was talking about days during fall camp when the team would have two practices. He told the coaches and players that finding the energy for one practice is easy—the challenge is doing it a second time. This really hit home to me then, and even more so as I prepared to run seven marathons in seven days on seven continents. First, I ran one, then I did two in a row! If I could do that, I could do seven. And why not seven in seven days? I do not know the answer, but I knew if I didn't try, I would never know. The only way to find out was to take on the challenge—just like I took on my education and work. I worked the hustle mindset that I learned from Coach.

In 2013, when I was with the Washington Huskies, we were having an amazing season. After a win over the Oregon State Beavers and an Apple Cup victory against the Washington State Cougars, our head coach, Steve Sarkisian (Coach Sark), left the University of Washington when he was offered the head job in his home state at USC. This was a great opportunity for him, but the season wasn't over yet for us. Transition is hard for any organization because people who have been involved so deeply are left with a lot of questions and very few answers. It reminds me of something a coach once told me, "Be the answer." In other words, I should stay calm so we could find a way to finish the season. For the first time, I wasn't the underdog. The support staff was looking at me to figure things out. I was the most senior person in the room and had the privilege to take the lead.

The first thing I did was call a staff meeting. It was the first time in my professional life that I took the lead. I decided the best approach would be to understand why I was there. What were we trying to do? That's easy. I was there to help the most important stakeholders in the room—the student athletes. They had invested a lot into their season, and they needed to have a great bowl experience. To make this happen, we had to come together as a support team. We acknowledged that we were in the middle of a difficult time, but we still had the power to make a positive impact on the student athletes. As the month went on, everyone was taking their roles and responsibilities to new heights. It was awesome to see. In the end, the team won the bowl game and after the season was finished, I got the opportunity to follow Coach Sark back to Los Angeles. This experience was another growth spurt for me—I began to see obstacles in a whole new way.

Coach also told us, "Do not just run plays to run plays." This meant that everything that we did as a team should have a purpose and move us closer to our goal. On the field, when we practiced situational football, we would look at specific scenarios that occurred during the game. I take the same approach to life. I make sure that I know why I am doing something and then commit to moving it forward.

I am proud of the success I have achieved in my football career: I was promoted at two universities and served as the director of football operations. But around this time, I noticed that my dream had started to change. While I loved and cared for the people around me, I felt pulled in a different direction. I couldn't stop thinking about the World Marathon Challenge (WMC). Once the idea was in my head, I couldn't let it go. I knew to do it right I would have to quit my job. As much as I loved my job, I had to know—did I have what it takes to run seven marathons in seven days on seven continents?

TRUST THE
PROCESS

TAKING

ON

THE WMC

I wanted to connect with something beyond me— something important that would help others.

TRUST THE PROCESS

In November of 2017, I participated in a student panel for the International Dyslexia Association (IDA). The amazing students on the panel were from Lakeridge High School, the home of football player and coach, Doug Nussmeier. They were so passionate about learning and demonstrating their knowledge, but school did not always give them an opportunity to do that, which was a big problem. They may not have been able to recall a specific item or fact, but the details and information they did learn were more applicable to the real world.

Before the panel started that day, the teachers participated in a dyslexia simulation. A simulation is a series of activities that give participants a sense of what it is like to have difficulties with reading, writing, visual-motor coordination, and copying from the board. While they experienced these challenges, I wonder if they thought about how the difficulties they experienced had nothing to do with their intelligence.

I hoped that they did, so they might understand the frustration of being intelligent but still having trouble in school because of dyslexia. The participants in the simulation said that they felt frustrated and wanted to leave the room, but for me and others who struggled to read, that was never an option. Instead, we suffered. But I am not complaining; those painful experiences gave me the strength to run and challenge myself in other ways, including the WMC.

After the panel discussion, I talked with a physical therapist whose two children have dyslexia. She asked how I was running seven marathons in seven days on seven continents. I explained that my experiences of growing up with dyslexia had a lot to do with taking on this challenge. I explained that all of those years of going from school to occupational therapy, eating in the car (and feeling nauseated!) to finishing my lunch before going back to school, attending soccer practice, and working with my tutor, was a kind of marathon too. All of these things helped me develop the stamina and resilience I needed to run the distance. And, my mom was my trainer! When she first learned that I was serious about the WMC, she thought it was a little crazy until I reminded her that she and my father had helped me train for it all of my life by expecting and insisting that I would succeed. I also told her I could do it because of the kids on the panel. They needed to know that they were not alone, just like me. I was here for them—and that gave me the strength and energy that I needed to keep going.

My dream of running in the WMC was always about more than achieving a personal goal. I wanted to connect with something beyond me—something important that would help others. I chose to work with the IDA because I believe in their mission and that the organization will change the culture of how people with dyslexia are treated in classrooms across the country and around the world. Running seven marathons in seven days on seven continents seemed like a good way for me to support the organization.

All of these motivating factors were central to my decision to take on the WMC, but I also knew the importance of training for it as an athlete. My coordination has always been a challenge, including when I run. Understanding the most efficient way to do something or knowing the proper technique does not come naturally to me. When I ran my personal best marathon of 3:02:14, my technique was inefficient, and my body was working against itself. My arms swung across my chest and my legs didn't come off the ground. However, it wasn't until I had a leg injury that I finally went to a movement lab in Los Angeles where they analyze your gait among other things to identify inefficiencies in technique. The physical therapist there showed me a few things about posture and form. This new knowledge helped me know my body better and changed my whole perspective on movement.

When I began practicing my new posture, even my walking became more efficient. I began to understand the mechanics of speed. When I moved back to Portland in July 2017, I found a movement specialist at Evolve Performance. We met regularly and started working on the lower leg injury and strengthening some body mechanics as well, starting with the toes and building strength through hips, core, and back. The leg injury was a symptom of weakness in other parts of the body, so we needed to strengthen my whole body. Before long, I was ready to run my first test simulation of the WMC.

I began this part of my training by running the San Francisco Ultramarathon, two back-to-back marathons in a single day. This race meant a lot to me, not only because it was the farthest I would run in a single day, but also because San Francisco is a special place for my family. My older brother Adam and his fiancée live there, and so did my grandparents.

The first marathon started at midnight, the night before my birthday, July 23, 2017. Running in the dark that night, I thought of my Grandpa Phil who patrolled the Golden Gate Bridge through the night when he was stationed there with the Navy. I also thought of my grandma and her family who settled in San Francisco after escaping from the Nazis. That night and the next day, when the members of my family were there to cheer me on, I felt more connected to my family than ever.

After San Francisco, I went to Seattle to run another marathon, running a total of three marathons in one week. This was forty percent of the distance that I would be running for the WMC.

At the same time, I continued to work on mechanics. Besides working with Evolve, I went to Northwest Foot and Ankle for help with my feet. I started using toe spacers and shoes that provided more room for my toes to lay flat. This would help my feet get stronger, more flexible, and hold up better on the road. For body mechanics I started working with Flex and Flow Yoga. Jamie King and her team helped me understand the poses and how to move in and out of postures. I also continued my strength work, but I added a day with Dana Katz's fitness group to make sure I was performing the exercises with correct form. We also discussed running in general.

Yassine Diboun started coaching me in September 2017. He and I had a phone call after I ran a marathon in Utah. It was a rough race, and I really felt like I needed some coaching from someone who had been there before. I had heard of Yassine and his training program, the Wy'east Wolfpack, from a friend of my sister-in-law, Maria Elena. Our conversation went well, and I immediately knew that it was a good fit. There's a quote from Damian Lillard's Instagram feed that I often use to describe myself: "Lions and tigers may be more powerful, but wolves do not perform in the circus." I was ready to join the pack. Yassine drew up the running training plan, and I did it, even though it included rest days, which made me angry and frustrated. But it was all part of the process, and I accepted that I needed to trust the process and practice patience.

After working with Yassine for a while, I had a cool moment on the track. He told me that my form looked efficient, which would be helpful for high mileage and stability. He had not seen me run before all of the work that I had been doing on body mechanics. Then it hit me: this is what it takes for me to go forward and progress in anything I want to do—relentless effort and the pursuit of excellence in all things leading to my ultimate goal. It was like my parents taking me to all of those testing places, the hours and hours spent with tutors and occupational therapists, learning about dyslexia, and everything else that went into my education. The formula is the same for any challenge I face, whether it's learning to read or preparing to run the WMC. I am good at taking on challenges. I pour everything I have into it, and I cover all the bases, which is how I knew that I still needed to work on one more piece of the formula: fuel.

Fuel has always been a challenge for me. Occupational therapy activities had nauseated me. I would eat, but it didn't always feel good. And sometimes, because I was so focused on my schoolwork, I would forget to eat and skip meals because I didn't want to take the time to do it. I'd tell my parents, "Don't worry. I'll eat as soon as I finish my homework." I worked through the hunger. I just didn't want to take the time to eat— I felt like I needed to be doing something more productive. But to run the WMC, I would need to make the time to eat because how you fuel has a tremendous impact on performance. So, with the help of my coaches and nutritionists, I was able to build a plan for fueling. It became a critical part of my training regimen; I relied on it, especially during races. Finally, all the pieces were beginning to fall into place.

THE WMC
AND TAKEAWAYS

Part of this journey was about opening up and getting comfortable with being uncomfortable, especially when it came to sharing my experiences with dyslexia.

THE WMC AND TAKEAWAYS

The journey to the WMC race began on January 24, 2018, when I left Portland for Cape Town, South Africa. The weekend prior, IDA published a press release to the local news affiliates, so I was receiving calls from the media for interviews. I was grateful for this opportunity to share my story and talk about TeamQuest and IDA. This was my *why* for running. It was also making the challenge feel more and more real. I imagined that it was how professional fighters felt at the press conference and weigh-in before a title fight. Part of this journey was about opening up and getting comfortable with being uncomfortable, especially when it came to sharing my experiences with dyslexia. I was so thankful that people took interest because it was my privilege to shine a light on learning challenges and the impact they have on students.

To get to South Africa, I boarded a flight from Portland to Seattle. The moment I left Portland, my mindset was "beast mode on." I had wanted to run this race for three years, so I was focused and determined. From Seattle, it was on to Dubai, a fifteen-hour flight. I had a long layover in Dubai, but fortunately, there was a hotel in the airport—it was really convenient. I went from the plane, through security check, and then straight to the hotel. I was determined to stick to my plan of getting a nice treadmill workout at the hotel to break things up in between flights. I always needed to be "in motion," and it was even more critical for maintaining my composure as I prepared for race day. The flight from Dubai to South Africa was only ten hours.

On January 28, all fifty competitors met as a group at the Cape Town Westin Hotel. Being in that room was so surreal for me. I had been thinking of this moment for three years. I could feel the energy, while still being nervous, excited, and everything else in between. I was called to get my race packet and bib number—one step closer to the race. The next day, we had the briefing for the Antarctica race. The first time I had ever had a comparable pre-planning meeting for a race was the day before the San Francisco Ultramarathon. It was such a great moment for me because the San Francisco race had been part of my training for the WMC. My family had been there with me, strategizing the course. They weren't at this meeting in South Africa, but I sensed their presence. I felt encouraged and confident that my preparation was already paying off, even before the race had started.

The night before the race in Antarctica, I had a terrible time sleeping. I am not sure if it was excitement, nerves, or simply not wanting to miss the morning charter. I would sleep for a couple of hours and then get up and stretch, send out some last-minute messages to my tribe, and check my gear. I also sat in the stillness of the hotel and mentally visualized the race. I actually like being awake during a time when the rest of the world is asleep. Things became clear to me in the quiet. I thought back to grade school when I had to work harder and longer than others to get ahead and achieve. Nothing had changed. Knowing this also helped my confidence levels. It confirmed that my plan of attack and drive were still similar to when I was a kid. And besides, I knew if I needed to rest, I would have a ten-hour plane ride later to make up that time.

It was five degrees Fahrenheit with wind chill in Novo, Antarctica. I had to adapt to the course being hot (yes, even in Antarctica it gets hot when the sun reflects off the snow!) on one side and cool on the other. I had to take off clothes for one half of the course and layer up on the other. One half of the course had a slight incline, the other a slight decline. However, the decline side had a strong headwind, so I had resistance on both sides of the course. But it was so peaceful in its isolation—listening to the sound of my feet hitting the snow.

Toward the end of the race, the fuel-up stations ran out of water, but I remembered my training—even when things are not ideal, you need to go with it and make the best of the situation. Finishing that race, I was tired and felt that I had worked hard. It was a good feeling after race number one. My final tally was 4:05:12. I had started the WMC.

The race in Cape Town, South Africa was much warmer at seventy-five degrees. This race had its own challenges. My group ended up running an extra mile due to a misdirection on the course, but I worked to stay cool (literally and figuratively) and positive. The sun was a challenge, and I have struggled in past races with running in warmer temperatures. When the race began to fall apart (my time wasn't what it should be), I saw an aid station and thought a cola might help. Perhaps my body would respond well to the sugar. I decided against it because I had not done that in a race before, even though these were not normal conditions. After the race, one of the competitors told me that he was struggling as well and had started alternating between water and cola, which helped him. It was hard to know when to make adjustments when you plan for something so extensively. Drinking soda during a marathon seemed like such a bad idea. Part of me thought it best to stick to my plan, while the other part of me knew it could be good to adjust and adapt. From that point on, I decided to be more adjustment-focused with the goal of accepting the consequences. I finished the race in 4:27:53.

In Perth, Australia, my goal was to run a smooth and consistent race. Unfortunately, I started to have pain in my left leg during the race. I wasn't able to massage it out. By mile twenty-two, it locked up completely. Every stride was painful to the point that I wanted to vomit each time I took a step. I decided to walk but was heartbroken because I had put so much work into this race. Another competitor reminded me that I just needed to finish and focus on making it to the next race. He was 100% right. I had to deal with the disappointment.

It helped to think about when I worked with Pete Carroll and Coach Sark. They had a twenty-four-hour rule for thinking about the previous game (positives and negatives). After twenty-four hours, you had to forget that game and move on to the next. I applied that rule to the four miles I walked and for half the night. That night I talked to my brother Adam and Coach Yassine Diboun. Their conversations and my training helped with this process as well. I accepted that I did not achieve the results that I wanted and figured out how to process and get ready for the next session. So, by settling into the disappointment, I could turn my attention to the positives and go on. I finished the Perth race in less than five hours and had enjoyed the company of a group that was listening to music and had a lot of positive energy, making it a fun experience. This race also gave me insight to my new norm of what running could be like with my leg. It was just another new challenge. I've been through so many already in my life, what was one more? I finished in 4:46:20.

Now I was in Dubai, Asia. I adapted yet another new mindset for the race. In yoga, everything was about being open and accepting where your body is. So, my mindset was simple: Finish Dubai and get to Lisbon, Portugal! Anything is possible when you move "inmotional" (*emotion plus movement*). But after twenty-three miles of smooth running, my knee locked again. As frustrating as it was, this time I had a plan. I also remembered something from college: continuing my education after high school was very important to me, but after I finished college, it was not as fulfilling as I had hoped. For me, it was more about chasing the goal than the results. My goal was to become a stronger competitor and person. Sure, I was disappointed when I didn't meet my own high expectations—but I do my best to go on and move forward. My mindset in Perth was devastation and heartbreak. My mindset in Dubai was work in the new circumstance to the best of my ability. This is only the beginning. When asked if I was going to continue dragging my leg, there was no question in my mind. Of course! Beast Mode On! I finished in 4:42:47.

In the Lisbon race in Europe, I decided to work on a new strategy because of the conditions. The course was cobblestones, wood, and road. It was very different from the other races so far. The changes in surfaces were going to be a challenge, especially with the problems I was having with my leg. I started the race super conservatively. I would let myself run, and then when my knee started to lock, I would walk. In ultraraces, sometimes people power walk up hills to conserve energy. I thought about doing that when my knee started to go as I was approaching a hill. This strategy worked until about mile twenty-one when it locked completely. The last five miles, I was dragging that leg. Fortunately, my older brother Josh was there, and he and I finished the last lap together. He never left me: he trekked on, carrying all of the stuff that he had brought with him for the trip. I maintained that positive mindset with the focus of getting to South America. I finished in 5:25:59.

The WMC had become a battle to stay motivated, focused, and energized, so I developed an analogy to help. In a lot of professional sports in the United States, such as baseball, hockey, and basketball, playoffs and championships are typically seven-game series. One team must win four of the seven games to advance and win. If I thought about the WMC in the same way, I had done well in Antarctica and South Africa. Perth, Dubai, and Lisbon had been tough races where

I did not complete the races at my best. So, going into South America, I was down two games to three. This was like Kobe Bryant and the Lakers going back to Los Angeles down three games to two against the Celtics in 2010. I was making my way back home, and all I had to do was win the next two. I still had the chance to flip the script and make this one heck of a story. I talked with my trainer Rob Scheidegger upon arriving in Cartagena, Colombia. We developed a strategy for physically releasing pressure in the leg. It was a painful process, yet effective.

Two miles into the run in Cartagena, I completely ate it and fell on the ground. I had dirt on my face and scrapes on my arms. I immediately thought about all the times I had fallen in training, especially on a thirty-mile workout on Wildwood Trail in Forest Park near Portland. I got up and started moving the wrong way and then was corrected by another runner and kept going. I caught up to a fellow runner, JP, whom I had run with in South Africa, and we ran together. At the water stops he would fuel up and hydrate, and I would release pressure in my leg. We finished the race together tied for fifth. I counted this one as a strong finish. I had tied the series three to three and was headed home to finish my story in Miami, Florida. Race time: 4:14:02.

In Miami, I ran my heart out to keep up with the third-place pack. My family was in attendance and with the last lap, I went deep into the zone to pull it out. I spent everything I had. My leg felt completely locked up, and I remembered my coach telling me I could plant it and run off it. So, that is what I did and found enjoyment through the pain. Seeing my family at the finish line was so special for me. After the race, I took a moment to congratulate other participants and then I headed back to the hotel with my family.

My family was concerned that I hadn't eaten very much so they ordered room service, while I immediately went to the bathtub to take a hot soak with Epsom salt. It's funny—people ask me what I did once I finished. Yes, I did celebrate with my family, but my immediate thought was to recover, and that bath was the only thing on my mind.

I remember thinking that the race was over, but my mindset and mentality of preparation and strategy would never be over. I got into the tub, and even though the water was warm, I was shaking. It was so crazy to me that I had finished the challenge and it was over. When I came out of the tub, the food had arrived, and my family had left the room. It would have been hard to explain that I wasn't too hungry, so I'm glad it was just my brother in the room. I was so shocked at having completed the race that I think the adrenaline had hindered my appetite. I tried to snack a little purely for the benefit of my body, but I also found it hard to turn down chips and guacamole. How could I turn that down? An hour later I went to dinner with my family at a restaurant. Still not hungry, I just enjoyed having my family all there together. I am so grateful and fortunate that I had this opportunity. But it is only the beginning; I am just getting started. I finished tied for third overall with a time of 4:03:36.

AFTERWORD

For a very long time, I was afraid to talk about my dyslexia. I thought it was something to hide. Over time, I've learned that dyslexia is actually very common, but getting the instruction needed to overcome it isn't—especially in the public schools. I want to do something about that. That's why I am sharing my story. Although it was scary for me to use my voice, it scared me more to think about *not* using my voice. Students who struggle need to know they are not alone. I want to be a resource for them, their parents, and teachers. While I am naturally more of a listener, and sharing is an entirely different approach for me, I will continue to share my story as long as it helps others. Thanks for the love and support that I have had along the way; I have been able to accomplish many things. If I can do the same for others by making their journey easier, then I have a responsibility to do that—and it is something I want to and will do.

Dyslexia can be a superpower. It demands mindful, daily practice, and it has given me the stamina and resilience that I needed to succeed in school, at work, and in my life. What can it do for you?

ACKNOWLEDGMENTS

I have tried my best to acknowledge each person who has played a pivotal role in my story, or who has helped me tell my story. Unfortunately, space limitations prevent me from mentioning everyone. I have been fortunate to know so many people over the years who have truly inspired me, and I want to at least mention a few of them by name. Please know there are many more I have not mentioned who also have helped me and given me life lessons. I am so grateful.

First, a special thank you to my amazing family!

To my sister, Alexis Blank—her strength and independence were a constant stream of inspiration.

My brother, Adam Blank, gave me someone to look up to. I could not have asked for anything more from him.

My brother's partner in crime, Molly Stark, supported me from the first time I met her and makes one heck of a sister.

My brother, Josh Blank, showed me what it meant to show up in life. He is one of the best at that.

Maria Elena—she is what our family calls a god-send, and she lives up to that daily.

My parents, Owen and Lynn Blank—there are really no adequate words to thank them. My dad taught me what it means to be a man. Anything good that comes my way is because of his coaching and teaching. My mom is one of the strongest people I know. Her determination and grit have motivated me throughout my life.

My nieces, Aliyah and Carmen Blank—it has meant so much connecting with you on this project from videos to coaching in the pool. I am so excited to see you grow and develop. Love you both so much!

To Erin, Jack, and Ryan—thank you for reminding us what it means to have energy and love for one another. I'm here for you all!

Miguel De La Rosa, you believed in this project from the get-go—from the day we met—and it was like we were brothers.

Ishaan Vadhera, you were a constant reminder that sometimes you need to push to do good in this world.

Mike Francis, you were the catalyst and motivation for this story to be written.

Ryan Magsino, you really made this story come to life through your creative artwork.

Alex Rios, thank you for your assistance with digital marketing and production.

To my training partner overseas—Luke Tyburski, thank you for the constant motivation and understanding. You supported me from the day we met. I'm thankful for that, and we will run a race together someday!

Jon Spoelstra, for brainstorming this book concept with me and editing along the way.

Conor Knowles, for being a sounding board for a long time and editor of this book. He believed in me and the dream of running seven-seven-seven.

Zach Hermsen, for giving me the opportunity to talk to his class about learning challenges.

Yogi Roth, for constantly pushing me to think bigger and sharing the book *The Alchemist* with me! And, thank you for all the surf sessions.

To Carly, Henry, and Toby Ruggiero—you have been family to me. Living with you all in Seattle was truly something that I am grateful for. Now, watching you raise your own family has been magical.

My performance team: Yassine Diboun, Rob Scheidegger, Carl Baird, and Dr. Michelle Gilpin.

Robyn Hefner for helping me prepare for my first marathon in 2010.

Northwest Foot and Ankle, especially Camden Allison-Hall.

Jamie King and her team at Flex and Flow Yoga.

Aunty Sushi.

And, thank you to anyone who has ever been my teacher! Especially Mrs. Gronquist, Paige Chandler, Margaret McNabb, David Bailey, and so many more!

To Rachel Ebbers and her team at Fleet Feet Sports.

Jane Cooper, Danielle Thompson, and Elizabeth Dove, from the Oregon Branch of IDA; Sonja Banks, Megan Davis, and Patrick Thorton from the home office of IDA. Patrick, thank you for picking up my call! And, thank you to my editor, Denise Douce, at the home office of IDA for her commitment, dedication, and enthusiasm. I am so grateful for her contribution.

CPSIA information can be obtained
at www.ICGtesting.com
Printed in the USA
JSHW011348280121
11210JS00005B/116

9 780892 140725